LINUX

Beginners guide for learning Linux & Shell scripting

Table of Contents

Introduction

I want to congratulate you for buying this book as well as encourage you to read it, as it will represent the best

3

source of information about Linux. If you want to understand how Linux works and get to the next level with your computer, you made the right decision to buy this book.

Shell scripts are an essential part of any modern operating system, such as UNIX, Linux, Windows and other similar systems. The scripting language may vary from one OS to another, but the fundamental principles remain the same. My first contact with Linux Shell scripts was during the development of embedded Linux product.In this first encounter, Shell scripts initialized the complete product from basic booting procedure until users logged in and a complete operating system was initialized. Another situation was in the automation of regular activities, such as the build and release management of source codes of very complex products, where more than 5,000 les were a part of a single project.

In this book, you will learn about the basics of Shell Scripting to a more complex customized automation. After reading this book you will be able to create and use your own shell scripts for the real-world problems out there. The book is designed to be as practical as possible and to give you the look and feel of Linux world at the best.

the owned by the owners themselves, not affiliated with this document.

Chapter 1: Getting started with shell scripting

At the end of this chapter you will know how to:

- Make a comparison of shells and how they work.
- Have a basic understanding of Linux commands and also be familiar with commands.
- Differentiate when to use scripts and when not to.
- Write your first script in Linux.
- What are the permissions, and how to work with them.

- Get things done in an effective way.
- And much more!

When starting to work with Linux you will come across shell as the first program to work with.

The shell represents a program which provides direct access to the operating system. Let's take a look at Linux evolution and how this operating system has evolved over time.

Linux represents a Unix-like computer operating system. Linux was released on 17 September 1991 by Linus Torvalds. It was assembled under the model of free and open-source software. What made Linux so amazing and loved by users is the *Linux Kernel.* The Linux kernel represents a monolithic Unix-like computer system kernel, that belongs to the family of the operating system that is based on kernels. Android operating system for smartphones, for instance, it's also based on the Linux kernel. Because of that, we can, therefore, say that Linux is an operating system kernel. The free software foundation that Linux is being part of uses the name of GNU/Linux.

When Torvalds created Linux the intention was to use it for personal computers. They wanted it to be developed on the Intel x86 architecture but the original plans changed and since that moment of creation, Linux has been ported to more and more platforms which made it be very popular. When Android dominance started taking root on smartphones and tablets things changed in Linux world. In this particular moment, Linux is one of the leading systems used in servers and mainframe computers.

Let's get started!

- **Different types of shells and their comparison**

Bourne shell is the shell program that is used on Unix OS. Let's take a look at the following categories representing a brief information about different shells:

- Csh – C Shell was created by Bill Joy in 1970, it's a Unix Shell

- Tcsh – it is the C Shell with the programmable command line. Competition, command line editing and a couple of more features define Tcsh.

- Ksh – Korn Shell is a Unix Shell developed by David Korn in the early 1980s.

- Bash – GNU Bourne Again Shell it's one of the most common shell. Is a command language developed by Brian Fox released in 1989. Bash is distributed as the default login shell for Linux distributions.

14

Let's take a look at some features for a couple of shells:

Aliases : C, TC, Korn, Bash

Command-line editing: TC, Korn, Bash

Functions: Bourne, Korn, Bash

Spelling correction: TC, Bash

Prompt formatting: TC, Bash

Functions of the Shell

It doesn't matter what we type in the shell terminal, the shell will take the command and executive. Here we can take a look at a couple of activities done by the shell:

- Text reading and parsing the entered command.

- The shell takes care of signal handling.

- Evaluation of meta-characters like wildcards and special characters.

When it comes to working with the shell you will get started by opening the terminal on your computer. Start working with different commands and get used to Linux terminal. After opening Linux terminal start by typing:

$ echo $SHELL

/bin/bash

What we have typed says in the terminal that the current shell is /bin/bash such as BASH shell:

$bash –version

GNU bash, version 2.05.01 – released (i386 –redhat –linux gnu)

When working with Linux you will discover that filenames in lowercase and uppercase are different. For example, the files "Hi" and "hi" are different files in

Linux. It's a little different from other operating systems where case does not make a difference. As you may see on Windows computers or Mac computers. Avoid also using spaces in filenames or directory. Take a look at the following example:

- Wrong way to name a file: Hi user.txt

- Good way to name a file: Hi_user.txt or Hiuser.txt

If you are not naming correctly a file that you are working with, that file will not respond. Also, some utilities and commands will fail.

Advice: For working with Linux faster use tab completion feature. It helps a lot when typing in filenames or directory names.

- **Basic commands used when working with Linux**

- $ ls = ls command used to view what is inside the directory that you are working with. Also used if you want to find out information about a file.

- $ls –a= ls-a command to see hidden files.

- $ pwd = 1. This command helps to check the present working directory.

2. Used also to verify if we have moved to the directory that we are looking for.

- $ cd work = cd work command will change the working directory to the created directory.

- $ mkdir = This command creates a new directory for you.

- $ touch hi.sh = the command "touch" is used when we want to create a new empty file. In this situation is called hi.sh, located in the current folder.

- $ ll = the ll command has the purpose of displaying information about the files.

- $ rm= rm is the command that will delete a selected file.

- $ rm .welcome.sh = this command will delete the file welcome.sh

Now that we have a basic understanding of Linux commands we are going to start working on our first script. We are going to create our first script and we are going to call it Welcome.sh.This time round for creating a script you can use any text editor that you want the important thing is to type commands correct.

- **Script Creation**

1. Let's create a new hello.sh file :

```
#! /bin/bash

# command line

echo " Welcome"

ls

date
```

2. Save the file that you've created:

We wrote a script using the commands that you saw. The #! /bin/bash is a shebang line. Any line that it's starting with # will be considered a comment line expecting the first line #! /bin/bash.

- The "echo" command will display "Hello World" on your monitor.
- The "ls" command will display directory content.
- The "date" command will display date and time.

Execution of newly created commands can be done in the following ways:

1. $ bash hello.sh

2. $ chmod +x hello.sh

The result is adding new executable permission to our newly created file. We will talk more about that in the following pages.

$ ./hello.sh

The output of the newly created commands:

Hello World
Hello.sh
Mon Feb 01 09:09:18 IST 2017-07-05

Creation of a more complex script

We will continue to create another script based on what we have already developed. The name of the script will be "helloAgain.sh":

```
#!/bin/bash
# Scriptname : helloAgain.sh
# Author: James Marshall

echo "Hello $LOGNAME, Wish you the best !"
echo "You're are working in directory `pwd`."
echo "You are working on a machine called `uname -n`."
```

24

```
echo "List of files in your
directory is."
ls       # List files in the present
working directory
echo   "Bye $LOGNAME. The
time is `date +%T`!"
```

Output after executing "helloAgain.sh":

Hello student, Wish you the best !
You are working in directory /home/student/work.
You are working on a machine called Raspberry Pi.
List of files in your directory is.
hello1.sh hello.sh
Bye student. The time is 12:13:04!

Compiler and interpreter

In your program there are 2 options, compilation and interpreter:

Compilation: uses a compiler based language as Java, C , C++

Interpreter: uses languages as Bash Shell scripting.

Using a compiler-based language will compile the source code. The result of compilation is a binary executable file. The binary executable file can be executed to check performance.

When working with Shell script, such as an interpreter-based program, every line of the program is input to the Bash shell. The lines are executed sequentially. As a result, the first line will be executed by the shell interpreter. If the next line of the script has an error the previous line will still be executed.

Don't use scripts in the following situations

Shell scripting has its own limitations. There is no doubt that shell scripts have certain advantages over compiler-based programs. For a better use of shell scripts, I recommend taking a look at the advantages and disadvantages of shell scripts.

Part of the attributes that make shell scripting perform so good are as follows;

- The possibility to write scripts very easily.
- Scripts are very easy to start and no special training is needed.
- Scripts are easy for debugging.
- The fact that can save a lot of time for development.

- No additional setup or tools are required.
- The administration is automated.

Limitations of shell scripts

- Every new line creates a new process in the operating system.
- Execution of a compiled program runs as a single process for the program.
- Not good for heavy math operations.
- Shell scripts are slow compared to compiled programs.

There are also some definite situations where we can't use Shell scripts at all, like:

- When file operations are required.
- When data structures are needed (linked lists)
- When we need to generate or manipulate graphics.
- When direct access is needed to system hardware.
- When we need a port or socket I/O.

28

- When we need an interface with legacy code.

Diverse directories

Let's explore the directory structure in Linux:

/bin/ : The bin directory contains commands used by the user.

/boot/ : The boot directory contains the files required for operating system start-up.

/cdrom / :The cdrom directory makes the CD-ROM files accessible.

/dev / : The dev directory keeps the device driver files. Those files are used for running hardware-related programs using kernel.

/etc / : The etc directory contains configuration files and startup scripts.

/home / : The home directory contains a folder for all users, except the administrator.

/lib / : The lib directory stores the library files.

/media / : The media directory is used for external media such a USB Flash Drive.

/opt/ : The opt directory contains the optional packages that are installed there.

/proc/: The proc directory contains files that give information about the kernel.

/root/ : The root directory is representing the administrators home folder.

/sbin/ : This directory contains commands used by the administrator.

/ usr/ : The usr directory Contains programs, libraries and different documentation.

/ var/: The var directory has variables like http or tftp .

/ sys/: The sys directory creates dynamically sys files.

- **Working more effectively with shell**

One of the most used commands in Linux are "man","echo", "cat".

Entering the command $ man will show you various types of manual pages.

a. User commands
b. System calls
c. Library calls
d. Special files
e. File formats
f. Games
g. Miscellaneous
h. System admin
i. Kernel routines

When entering the man command with a specific number it will display one of the above types. As follows:

$ man 2 command

$ man 4 command

If we need to know more about the password command we can type the commands as follows:

$ man command

    man –q passwd
    man –Q passwd

$ man passwd

The first line will show all pages with that specific keyword. The second line will help you search all manual pages that are respecting a pattern.

You will get a good understanding of how this command works in the following situation:

$ whatis passwd

The output to our request is:

passwd(1ss1)
passwd(1)
passwd(5)

The first line has the purpose to compute password hashed. The second line has the purpose to change the user password. The last line has the purpose to change the password file.

! Note : Keep in mind that every command that we type in the terminal has an executable binary program. Each program has a file associated with it. For checking the location of a binary file it's recommended to use the following:

$ which passwd
usr / bin / passwd

As you may think the command above is used to tell us where is located in /usr/bin/passwd folder.

For displaying the user name of the current user we use the following command:

$ su

"su" command, or switch user, will give you possibility to get switch access form user to administrator.

To list all all declared names that are registered, we use the command:

$alias

To remove a declared user you do it by using the command:

$ unalias copy

For checking the operating system details or the distribution that is currently installed we use the following command :

$ uname

Output: The current operating system

If you are interested in finding out all the information's about your Linux computer, we use the following command :

$ uname –a

Linux has more types of files. To find out more about the type of file that you are currently using I suggest to check the following list:

Regular file (-)
Soft link(l)
Socket file (s)
Pipe file(p)
Character device driver(c)
Directory (d)

To get all information about a file, use the next command:

$file name_file

Output: will show the type of the command.

- **Working with permissions**

There are 3 types of permissions:

- Read permission: The user can read the content of the file.
- Execute permission: The user can execute the file he/she is currently using.
- Write permission: The user can modify or take action on a specific file.

Changing file permissions

First, you have to check the file permission by using the following command:

$ ll file_name

Command chmod

For changing the file or directory permission we can do it in two ways :

1. The symbolic method: This technique will add read and write permissions to the file that you are using. Adding "g" will be

related to the group and adding "o" will be related to others:

$ chmod ugo+ rwx file_name or $ chmod + rwx file_name

2. The numeric method: This method will change the file permissions using the octal technique:

$ chmod+rwx file_name

Unmask

Unmask command will show you how Linux decides the default permissions of the created file:

$ unmask
0002

The output "0002" has the following meaning: by creating a new directory the permission "0002" will be subtracted. For the new directory, the permissions will be 775 or rwx rwx r-x.

Setuid

The setuid feature is another feature very frequently used. If the bid of this feature is set for a script, as a result the feature will run the owner privileges. If the administrator wants to run a script wrote by himself then he/she has to set the bit of the feature.

Setgrid

This feature is similar to Setuid. Segrid gives the user the capacity to run scripts with group owner's privileges even if they are executed by another user.

$ chmod g+s filename or $ chmod 5500 filename

Sticky bit

The sticky bit is one of the most interesting functionalities that you will find in Linux. Let's take the following situation. A department has around 8 users. If a folder has been set with "sticky bit" then all users can copy files from that folder. Pretty useful when you need a quick and easy access, it also gives the possibility to other users just to read. You can control who can edit and modify the document also with "Sticky bit".

$ chmod +b file or $ chmod 2100

After preceding with this command the file permission will be drwxrwxrwt.

In this chapter, we have talked about ways to work with Shell scripts, different commands and how to handle Linux in general. In the next chapter, we will get deeper into learning about process management, automation among many other things.

Chapter 2: Process management, automation and job control

In this chapter you will familiarize yourself with the following topics:
- Job management – how to check processes and how to create jobs.
- Exploring the crontab.
- Monitoring processes.

Let's talk about the process basics

In Linux world for instance, running a program represents a process. When a program stored starts executing, then, as a result, the program has been created and is running.

Linux operating system boot-up sequence:

1. In personal computers, the BIOS chip initializes system hardware, display device drives and all pieces of hardware required.

2. Right after that, the BIOS executes the boot loader program.

3. Kernel is being copied. After some normal and basic checks, it calls a function names "start_kenel()".

4. After initializing the operating system the kernel creates the first progress, "init". For checking the presence of this process you can use the following command :

   $ ps -ef

5. The process ID of the "init" process gets the numerical identification "1". This is representing the parent process

of all user space processes. Every new process is created by "fork()". We can take a look at the process tree using the command:

$ pstree

You can see the very first process as "init" and also all other processes with a complete parent and child relation between them. By using the $ps -ef command, we will see that "init" process is owned by root and its parent process ID.

Three different types of processes:

Zombie process

All processes have one data structure called "process control table". The process control table is maintained in the operating system. The table contains the information about all the child processes created by the parent process. If the parent process is suspended or interrupted by any other reason the child process is terminated. The child process can't operate without the parent process. The parent process cannot receive the information about the child process termination. When this situation occurs we call it "zombie process". After the parent process awakes, it receives a signal about the child process termination. As a result, the process block data structure will be updated. Finally, the child process termination is complete.

Orphan process

If there is a situation where the parent process is terminated, the child process becomes an orphan process. The process that created the parent process is called "grandparent process". The grandparent process becomes the parent of the orphan child process. The "init" process becomes the parent of the orphan process.

Finally, the "orphan process" is complete.

Daemon process

We have started all processes in the Bash terminal. We will see that there are specific processes that are not associated with the terminal or any terminal in general. If we print any text with the $ echo "Hello" command it will print in the terminal as we are used. The processes that are not associated with any terminal are called "daemon process". Those type of processes are running in the background. Daemon processes are immune to any change that happens to the Bash Shell. Daemon processes are very useful when we want to run background processes. DHCP server is one of the background processes that make daemon processes very helpful.

Monitoring processes

Monitoring processes is done using the command ps. Let's talk more about that:

- To list process associated with our current Bah shell terminal enter the command :
  $ ps

- To list process along with the parent process ID, we use the command:
  $ ps -f

- To list processes with parent process ID along with the process state, we use the next command:
$ ps -lf

- For listing all the processes running on the operating system we use the command:
$ ps -ef

To find a particular process, you can use the following command:

$ ps –ef | grep "name_process"

- If we need to close or terminate a running process we use the following command:

$ kill name_of_process_to_be_killed

If the process is not terminated by the $kill command we can pass additional option to ensure that the process is killed:

```
$                kill                -9
name_of_the_process_to_kill
```

To find out more information about flags of the kill I recommend you to you use the command:

```
$ kill –l
```

This command will display all the signals or software interrupts used by the operating system. The $kill command sends the SIGTERM signal to the process.

- **Process Management**

Due to the fact that we already have a better understanding of how to check processes, will talk more about managing different process:

- In Bash Shell, any new command will start running in the foreground. As a result, we can't run more than one command in the foreground. To start more processes, we need to create many terminal windows. The processes will work as background processes.

- For starting a process in the background we need to do it by entering "&" in the Bash Shell.
- If you want to have your "Hello" program as a background process you can do it by entering: "$ Hello &"
- Terminating any command by "&" will make it run as a background process.

Taking the sleep command for example. If we issue this command we will create a new process. This process sleeps for the mentioned duration in the integer value:

1. To make the process sleep for 500 seconds will use the command :

$ sleep 500

As a result will not be able to use any other command from the terminal we used.

2. Pressing   CTRL   +   C combination will terminate the process created by the sleep command.

3. $ sleep 500 & for example will create a new process. This will put to sleep your computer for 500 seconds but it will start running in the background. Therefore, you will be able to enter the command in the Bash terminal.

4. Having a new process running in the background will make entering new commands very easy:

```
$ sleep 1000 &
$ sleep 5000 &
$ sleep 1000 &
```

5. Often we find our selfs in the situation where we have many processes running in the background. To check which processes are running you can do that by using the command:

```
$ jobs
```

The $jobs command has the purpose of listing all the processes running in the terminal. It will display foreground and also background processes. You can see their status as running, suspended or stopped. The job ID is mentioned in brackets []. + sign indicates which command will receive fg and bg commands by default.

6. Background processes that are already running can be made to run in the foreground. We can do that by using the following command:

$ fg 5

This means that job with number 5 will run from foreground instead of the background.

For making the process stop executing we press CTRL+Z. This shortcut will make suspend/ stop the foreground process. The process is stopped BUT NOT TERMINATED.

7. If you want to make the process stopped running in the background, use the command:

```
$ bg job_number
$ bg 5
```

This will make preceding command to suspend job number 5 to run in the background.

8. If you want to terminate the process one can do it by using job ID:

   $ jobs –l = command for listing jobs
   $ kill pid

- **Tools For Monitoring Process**

Linux gives you the possibility to track and view the performance of various processes in the operating system. You can do that by using different tools that we are going to discuss further. If you want to have a dynamic real-time view use the command "$ top". $ top command displays different information about the running system.

$ top command gives you information like:

- System update
- Current time
- Number of users logged in
- Load average

It also gives you information about hardware situation. For example CPU usage as being displayed as follows:

- * **us** (**user**): CPU usage in % for running (un-niced) the user processes.

- * **sy** (**system**): CPU usage in % for running the kernel processes.

- * **ni** (**niced**): CPU usage in % for running the niced user processes.

- * **wa** (**IO wait**): CPU usage in % for waiting for the IO completion.

- * **hi** (**hardware interrupts**): CPU usage in % for serving hardware interrupts.

- * **si** (**software interrupts**): CPU usage in % for serving software interrupts.

- * **st** (**time stolen**): CPU usage in % for time stolen for this vm by the hypervisor.

Also, you will get information about the memory usage of your computer which enables you to know a lot in regard to physical, used, and the available memory.

The following is a table of values that will help you to understand more about computer display;

- PID: This is the ID of the process.

- USER: This is the user that is the owner of the process.

- PR: This is the priority of the process.

- NI: This is the "NICE" value of the process.

- VIRT: This is the virtual memory used by the process.

- RES: This is the physical memory used for the process.

- SHR: This is the shared memory of the process.

- S: This indicates the status of the process: S=sleep, R=running, and Z=zombie (S)

- %CPU: This is the % of CPU used by this process.

- %MEM: This is the % of RAM used by the process.

- TIME+: This is the total time of activity of this process.

- COMMAND: This is the name of the process.

Let's look at the most important performance monitoring tools :

- Iostat
- Vmstat
- Sar

Statistics are very important. If you want to check statistics of CPU and also INPUT / OUTPUT utilization of the device you can use the following command:

$ iostat

$iostat –c

If you want CPU statistics only use the command: $ iostat –d

To check the virtual memory statistics we use the following command:

$ vmstat

$ vmstat –s

For showing different event counters and memory statistics use the command:

$ vmstat –t 2 6

Let's talk about time

For scheduling a task we have the "at" command at our disposal. From time to time we have to repeat a task. In this type of situations we use that "crontab" command but for scheduling a task at every day at a specific hour we use the "at" command.

The syntax is as follows: $ at time date

Examples of the at command :

```
$ at 8.45 AM
at > echo "Hi" > $HOME/inx.txt
at > Control + D
```

Control + D helps you to save the job. The code above means that the task will be executed at 8.45 AM. Will log a message to the inx.txt at 8.45 AM.

$ at 9 pm apr 19 2017
at > echo "list" | mail Susie
at > Control + D

The command above will send an e-mail on April 19, 2017, at 9 Pm to Susie.

- **Crontab**

    For running a specific task the solution is using "crontab" command.

The syntax of the command is as follows: $ crontab –e

This command will start by opening a director.

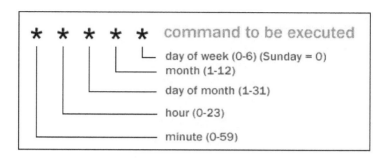

To save the process that you started is very easy :

save and quite crontab job

Below is a list of examples with the contrab command and how you can use it:

- Use the following command to run a script every 15 minutes, every day:

- **15 * * * * $HOME/bin/daily.job >> $HOME/tmp/out 2>&1**

- Use the following command to run 35

minutes after midnight every day:

- **35 * * * $HOME/bin/daily.job >> $HOME/tmp/out 2>&1**

- Use the following command to run at 9.35 P.M. on the first of every month—the output is mailed to John:

  35   04   1   *   *   *
  $HOME/bin/monthly

- Use the following command to run at 8 P.M. on weekdays, send the e-mail to john@gmail.com:

  0 20   *   *   1-5   sendmail
  john@gmail.com < ~/home/email.txt

- The sendmail utility is used for sending e-mails. We can use the mail utility also as follows:

**sendmail user@example.com
< /tmp/email.txt**

- The following commands are self-explanatory from the text of echo:

30 0-23/4 * * * echo "run 30 minutes after midn, 4 am, 6 am,

everyday

8 5 * * sun   echo "run at 8 after 5 every Saturday"

Chapter 3: Best text processing and filters to use

In the previous chapter, we talked about basic process management. In this chapter we are going to study more about the following topics:

- Working with grep.
- How to cut and paste.
- Input, output and what are standard errors.
- What are meta characters.
- How to work with comm, diff and uniq.

Usually, we can generate reports using Shell scripting and that is a very good aspect of Linux.That also includes processing different text files and filtering their output to get the result that you want. In order to understand more about this process, we are going to analyze two commands: **More** and **Less**.

More: In some situations, you will have to deal with very large quantities of output on your screen. This will happen for certain commands and those can't be viewed completely on a single screen. For those type of situations, we use the "more" command. This will help us to view the output text on the page at a time. All you have to do is to add "more" after the command:

$ ll / dev | more

This is what we call a pipe "|". The pipe is a very important element in Linux world and we are going to explore more on it in this book. Pressing Enter will move the screen by one line and space bar will make the output on one page at a time.

Less: Less is the command that will show you the screen full of text all at once. This command is a very useful text filtering tool.

Let's take a look at the syntax of this command:

```
$ command | less
$ ll / doc | less
```

We use this command for getting a long listing from the /doc folder. If you need to get information about a specific file is very simple. All we have to do is to use arrow key up or down to scroll. More command will help us to scroll backwards.

- **Head and tail**

For head and tail will have a practical exercise. In order to do our exercise will need a file with a sequence of numbers. Will have a sequence from 1 to 100 and for that, we will use the command:

$ seq 100 > numbers.txt

Head command helps us in creating a file having the numbers from 1 to 100 displayed. The numbers are displayed on separate lines. Below is an example with the "head" command:

$ head // will help you display first 10 lines.
$ head -5 numbers.txt // this command will help you to display the first 5 lines.
$ head +7 numbers.txt // will show numbers from line 7.

Tail command can be used by typing the following command:

$ tail // this command will display the last 10 lines
$ tail -2 numbers.txt // we use this command to display last 2 lines
$ tail +9 numbers.txt // this command will show numbers from line 9 onwards

Diff command

Diff command is a command used to search for difference between files. Let's take a look at the following examples for a better understanding.

We have a couple of documents to use. Doc1 has the following information:

I have to clean my room Sunday.
I sleep at noon Sunday.
I read for 15 minutes daily.

The Doc2 has the following information:

Tomorrow is Tuesday.
I have to clean my room Sunday.
I sleep at noon Sunday.
I read for 15 minutes daily.

The **diff** command comes in place:

$ diff Doc1 Doc2

The output of this command is as follows:

0a1
> Tomorrow is Tuesday.
The output 0a1 is indicating us that the content from the Doc1 is added to Doc2.

The content of Doc1 is as follows:

Tomorrow is Tuesday.
I have to clean my room Sunday.
I sleep at noon Sunday.
I read for 15 minutes daily.

The content of Doc2 is as follows:

Tomorrow is Tuesday.
I have to clean my room Sunday.
I sleep at noon Sunday.

$ diff Doc1 Doc2 is the command that will help you to get the next output:

4d3
< I read for 15 minutes daily.

In this situation, the output tells us that line number 4 is deleted from Doc 2.

The cut command

We use cut command for getting out specific columns from a text.

- -c: Will mention the filtering of characters.

- -d: Will mention the delimiter for fields.

- -f: Will mention the field number.

If you use for example this command

from etc/ passwd file first fields will be displayed. The image on your screen will show the login name, password and used Id:

$ cut –d: -f2-6 /etc/passwd

The join command

For this command will have a small exercise. For that, we are going to use the following files: file1.txt and file2.txt.

The content of file1.txt is as follows:

1 Spain
2 UK
3 Japan
4 US
5 Bulgaria

The content of file2.txt is as follows:

1 Barcelona
2 London
3 Tokyo
4 Washington
5 Sofia

The fields which have serial number are the same in both files. We can combine them with the command :

$ join file1.txt file2.txt

Output:

1 Spain Barcelona
2 UK London
3 Japan Tokyo
4 US Washington
5 Bulgaria Sofia

The paste command

As the name suggests the paste command has the purpose to paste two files horizontally. File1 will become the first column and File2 will become the second column:

$ paste File1 File2

The Uniq command

Below you have a couple of examples of the Uniq command:

This command removes duplicate lines from the file:

```
$ cat test
aa
aa
cc
cc
bb
bb
yy
zz
```

$ uniq test

This output removes the duplicate lines from test file, shown as follows:

aa cc bb yy zz

• The next command prints only duplicate lines:

$ uniq -d test

Output:

aa cc bb

The comm command

The comm command shows the lines to Doc1, Doc12 along with the common lines in them. We can use various options while using the command in the scripts:

$ cat Doc1

Barack Obama
Will Smith

Tony Robbins

$ cat Doc2
Barack Obama
Engela Merkel
Vladimir Putin
$ comm –nocheck-order file_1 file_2
Barack Obama
David Cameron
Jeff Bezos
Narendra Modi
Elon Musk

In the preceding example, we can note that :

• The first column shows unique lines in Doc1.

• The second column shows unique lines in Doc2.

• The last column shows the content common in both files.

The output shows that the unique les in file_1 are Will Smith and Tony Robbins.

Unique les in the second le are Jeff Bezos and Elon Musk. The command name in both the les is Barack Obama, which is displayed in the third column.

The tr command

The tr command is a Linux utility for text processing such as translating, deleting, or squeezing repeated characters, which is shown as follows: **$ tr '[a-z]' '[A-Z]' < filename**

- This will translate the lower case characters to upper case: **$ tr '|' '~' < emp.lst**
- This will squeeze multiple spaces into a single space: **$ ls –l | tr -s " "**
- In this example, the -s option squeezes multiple contiguous occurrences of the character into a single character. Additionally, the -d option can remove the characters. **Sort**: It sorts the contents of a text le, line by line.

- -n: Will sort as per the numeric value.

- -d: Will sort as per the dictionary meaning.

- -r: Will sort in the reverse order.

- -t: Option to specify a delimiter for fields.

- +num: Specifies sorting field numbers.

- -knum: Specifies sorting filed numbers.

- $ sort +4 sample.txt: This will sort according to the 4th field.

  - **File descriptors**

    All I/o are handled by the kernel. Either we are talking about files, pipes or sockets they are handled by kernel using a mechanism called file descriptor. A file descriptor integer maintained by the kernel and used by the kernel.

- **Redirection**

Once you have a file descriptor assigned to something different than a terminal, the result is called I/O redirection. The redirection is made by the shell to a file by closing the standard output file descriptor. After that, the descriptor is assigned to the file.

This command will take input from the sample.txt file:

$ wc < sample.txt

This command will take the content from the sample.txt file. "wc" command will print the number of lines, words in the sample.txt file.

$ echo "Hello world" > log.txt

The following command will redirect output and will be saved in the log.txt file:

$ echo "New document" >> log.txt

" > " Will replace the existing text in the log file. " >> " will append the text in the log file.

Example : $ tr '1 to 10' '1 to 100' < sample.txt

The summary of all I/O redirection commands will be as follows:

- **Brace expansion**

For specifying a set of characters we use curly braces. Curly braces allow you to automatically form all possible combinations of characters.

$ touch file{1,2,3}
$ ls

```
student@ubuntu:~/work$ touch file{1,2,3}
student@ubuntu:~/work$ ls
file1   file2   file3
student@ubuntu:~/work$
```

$ mkdir directory{1,2,3}{a,b,c}
$ ls

```
qrlecrolλjp  qrlecrolλ5s  qrlecrolλsc  qrlecrolλ3p
qrlecrolλj9  qrlecrolλjc  qrlecrolλ5p  qrlecrolλ39  qrlecrolλ3c
student@ubuntu:~/work$ ls
student@ubuntu:~/work$ mkdir directory{1,2,3}{a,b,c}
```

Pattern matching with the vi editor

For learning pattern matching, we will ensure that the pattern that we will search should be highlighted when the searched pattern is found.

The con guration le for vi is /etc/vimrc.

In the vi editor, give the following command to highlight search:

	Commands	Description
	:set hlsearch	This highlights search pattern
	:se[t] showmode	Show when you are in insert mode
	:se[t] ic	Ignore case when searching

	:set noic	Shows case sensitive search

Chapter 4: Start working with commands

In the previous chapter, we talked about different commands. We talked about Uniq, Less, More, tail command and many others. Standard input and output are other concepts that we covered in the previous chapter.

In this chapter we will cover the following topics:

- Analyzing shell and interpretation of commands.
- How to work with pipes.
- What are command separators and how to use them.
- And many other interesting topics.

- **Shell interpretation of commands**

After you log in, the $ sign will appear in your shell terminal. The Bash shell runs scripts as an interpreter. The Bash shell will read any type of command we type.

The Bash will read them as series of words called tokens. Each word that we have in the bash is separated by a space ( ) and semi colon (;). To terminate a command all we have to do is to press Enter key. After pressing Enter key a new line character will be inserted at the end of the command. In this situation, the first word is taken as a command. Consecutive words that follow are treated like parameters.

The shell processes the command line as follows:

- If applicable, substitution of history commands.

- Converting command line into tokens and words.

- Updating history.

- Processing of quotes.

- Defining functions and substitution of alias.

- Setting up of pipes, redirection, and background.

- Substitution of variables (such as $name and $user) is performed.

- Command substitution (echo `cal` and echo `date`) is performed.

- Globing is performed (file name substitution, such as rm *).

- Execution of the command.

The sequence of execution of different types of commands will be as follows:

- Aliases (l, ll, egrep, and similar)

- Keywords (for, if, while, and similar)

- Functions (user defined or shell defined functions)

- Built-in commands (bg, fg, source, cd, and similar)

- Executable external commands and scripts (command from the bin and sbin folder)

When a command is entered in the terminal, the command that is done will be "tokenized". After that, the shell will check if the command is alias.

- shell, therefore their execution is fast as compared to executable external commands or scripts. Executable external commands will have a corresponding binary le or Shell script le in the le system, which will be stored in any folder. The shell will search the binary le or script of a command by searching in the PATH environment variable. If we want to know what the type of command it is, such as if it is an alias or a function or internal command, it can be found out by the type built-in command, which is shown as follows:

•

```
$ type mkdir
mkdir is /bin/mkdir
$ type cd
cd is a shell builtin
$ type ll
ll is aliased to `ls -alF'
$ type hello

hello is a function
hello ()
{
    echo "Hello World !";
```

}
$ type for
for is a shell keyword

Checking And Disabling Shell Internal Commands

Bash has a provision of a few built-in commands to change the sequence of command line processing. We can use these built-in commands to change the default behavior of command-line processing.

• The built-in command will disable aliases and functions for the command which will be following the command. The shell will search for the external command and the built-in command will search for the command passed as an argument, as follows: **$ command ls** This will make aliases and functions be ignored and the external ls command will execute.

- The built in command will work as follows: **$ builtin BUILT-IN** This will ignore aliases and functions from the shell environment and only built-in commands and external commands will be processed.

- The break built-in command will work as follows: **$ builtin –n break** This will make the break built-in to be disabled and the external command break will be processed.

- To display all shell built-in commands,

94

give the command as follows:

$ enable

- The output on the screen will show the following as shell internal commands:

	c om man d	e val	h ist or y	p wd	e st
.	c omp gen	e xe c	j ob s	r ead	i m e s

[	c omp lete	e xit	k ill	r ead arra y	ra p
a lia s	c omp opt	e xp ort	l et	r ead onl y	r u e
b g	c onti nue	f als e	l oc al	r etur n	y p e
b in d	d eclar e	f c	l og ou t	s et, uns et	y p e s et
b re ak	di rs	f g	r ap fil e	s hift	li m it

b uil tin	di sow n	g eto pts	p op d	s hop t	m a s k
c all er	ec ho	h as h	p rin tf	s our ce	n al ia s
c d	e nabl e	h elp	p us hd	s usp end	ai t

• The shell built-in command can be disabled by the following:

$ enable –n built-in-command

For example: $ enable –n test In this case, in my shell, if we have to test an external command, then instead of the internal test command, the external test command will be executed.

The exit status

In Shell scripting, we need to check if the last command has successfully executed or not. For example, whether a le or directory is present or not. As per the result, our Shell script will continue processing.

For this purpose, the BASH shell has one status variable ?. The status of the last command execution is stored in ?. The range of numerical value stored in ? will be from 0 to 255. If successful in execution, then the value will be 0; otherwise, it will be non-zero, which is as follows:

$ ls

  $ echo $?

0

Here, zero as the return value indicates success.

In the next case, we see:

$ ls /root
$ echo $?
2

Command substitution

In the keyboard, there is one interesting key, the backward quote such as "`". This key is normally situated below the Esc key. If we place text between two successive back quotes, then echo will execute those as commands instead of processing them as plain text.

Alternate syntax for $(command) is the backtick character "`", which we can see as follows:

$(command) or `command`

For example:

- We need to use proper double quoted inverted commas, as follows:

- **$ echo "Hello, whoami"**

- The next command will print the text as it is; such as Hello, whoami:

- **Hello, whoami**

- Use proper double inverted commas:

- **$ echo "Hello, `whoami`."**

- **Hello, student**

- When we enclose whoami text in the "`" character, the same text which was printed as plain text will run as a command, and the command output will be printed on the screen.

- Use proper double inverted commas:

- **$ echo "Hello, $(whoami)."**

- **Hello, student.**

- Same like the earlier explanation.

Another example:

echo "Today is date"
Output:

Today is date

A similar example:

echo "Today is `date`"
Or:

echo "Today is $(date)"
Output:

102

Today is Fri Mar 20 15:55:58 IST 2015

- **Command separators**

Commands can also be combined in such a way that they are executed in a particular sequence.

Command1; command2

A command line can consist of multiple commands. Each command is separated by a semicolon, and the command line is terminated with a newline. The exit status is that of the last command in the chain of commands.

The rst command is executed, and the second one is started as soon as the rst one has finished.

$ w; date

Command grouping

Commands may also be grouped so that all of the output is either piped to another command or redirected to a le.

$ (ls; pwd; date) > outputfile

The output of each of the commands is sent to the le called out put file. The spaces inside the parentheses are necessary.

$ (w ; date) > whoandwhen

The output of the w command and date will be redirected to the whoandwhen le: **$ (echo "***x.c***";cat x.c) > log.txt** Output: This redirects the content of x.c with a heading ***x.c*** to the le out.

$ (pwd; ls; date) > log.txt

Output: This redirects output of commands pwd, ls, and date in the log.txt le.

- ### Logical operators

Let's now take a look at logical operators.

Command1 & command2

The first command is started in the

background to continue until it has finished; immediately after starting first command, the second command is started and it will run in the foreground:

$ find / -name "*.z" & s

---------------   -----

Command1 command2

In the preceding example, rst command such as nd will start running in the background and while the find command is running in the background, the ls command will start running in the foreground.

Command1 && command2

The second command is only started if the rst command is successful. To achieve this, the shell checks the exit (return) status of the rst command and starts the second command only if and when that exit status is found to be "0".

$ ls /home/ganesh && echo "Command executed successfully"
Since we are working as user ganesh,
$ ls /root && echo "Command executed successfully"

Since we are working as a normal user, we cannot access the /root directory. Therefore, nothing will be printed on the screen.

Command1 || command2

The second command is only started if the rst command fails. The shell checks the exit status of the rst command and starts the second command only if that exit status is not equal to "0".

$ ls /root || echo "Command execution failed"

Example:

$ ls || echo "command ls failed"

In the preceding example, if ls runs successfully, then echo will not be called. If the ls command fails such as $ ls /root and if the user is not root, then ls will fail and the echo command will print command ls failed.

When && or || are used, the exit status of the rst command is checked rst, then the decision to perform the next will be taken.

For example:

$ ls $ echo $?

0 $ ls /root

ls: /root: Permission denied
$ echo $?
1

$ tar cvzf /dev/st0 /home /etc | | mail -s "Something went wrong with the backup" root

If we give the command as follows:

$ cd /home/student/work/temp/; rm – rf *

Initially, the shell will change to the /home/student/work/temp folder, and then it will delete all les and folders.

- **Pipes**

We have already used pipes in many earlier sessions. It is a tool for inter-process communication.

$ command_1 | command_2

In this case, the output of command_1 will be sent as an input to command_2. The limitation is that the communication is a half-duplex. This means the data can move in only one direction. Normally for inter-process communication, you need to open les then get the le descriptor. This

108

will be used to write to the pipe le. Again, we need to create a Fifo le by special commands. The preceding technique simplifies all this process. We only need to insert "|" in between the two processes.

The operating system creates one intermediate buffer. This buffer is used for storing the data from one command and will be used again for the second command.

A simple example is as follows:

$ who | wc

The preceding simple command will be carried out in three different activities. First, it will copy the output of the who command to the temporary le. Then the wc command will read the temporary le and display the result. Finally, the temporary le will be deleted.

Normally, there will be two processes. The rst command is the writer process. The second process is the reader process. The writer process will write to temp_file and the reader will read from temp_file. Examples of writer processes are ps, ls, and date. Examples of reader processes are wc, cat, and sort.

Chapter 5: Expressions and variables

In the last chapter, you learned about how shell interprets any command, which is entered in the terminal or the command line. We also studied command substitution and separators in detail.

In this chapter, we will cover following topics:

- Working with environment variables.

- Exporting variables.

- Working with read-only variables.

- Working with command line arguments (special variables, set and shift, and getopt)

- Working with arrays.

- **Understanding variables**

    - Let's learn about creating variables in the shell. Declaring variables in Linux is very easy. We just need to use the variable name and initialize it with the required content. **$ person="Ganesh Naik"**

    ─ To get the content of the variable we need to pre x $ before the variable.

    For example:

    $ echo person
    person
    $ echo $person
    Ganesh Naik
    The unset command can be used to delete a variable:

    $ a=20

$ echo $a
$ unset a

The unset command will clear or remove the variable from shell environment as well.

$ person="Ganesh Naik"
$ echo $person
$ set

Here, the set command will show all variables declared in shell.

$ declare -x variable=value

Here, the declare command with the –x option will make it an environmental or global variable. We will understand more about environmental variables in the next sessions.

$ set

Again here, the set command will display all variables as well as functions that have been declared.

$ env

Here, the env command will display all environmental variables. **variable=value**

113

Whenever we declare a variable, that variable will be available in the current terminal or shell. This variable will not be available to any other processes, terminal, or shell.

- **Working with environment variables**

Environmental variables are inherited by any subshells or child processes. Every shell terminal has the memory area called environment. Shell keeps all details and settings in the environment. When starting a new terminal, the environment is created every time.

Let us have a look at environment variables by using the following command:

$ env

Or:

$ printenv

The local variable and its scope

In the current shell, we can create and also store user defined variables. These may contain characters, digits, and "_". A variable is not recommended to start with a digit. In general, for environment variables, upper case characters are used.

If we create a new variable, it will not be available in subshells. The newly created variable will be available only in the current shell. If we run Shell script, the local variables will not be available in the commands called by Shell script. Shell has one special variable $$. This variable contains the process ID of the current shell.

Let's try a few commands:

$ echo $$

1234

This is the process ID of the current shell.

$ name="Rob Jonson"
$ echo $name
Rob Jonson

We declared the variable name and initialized it.

$ bash

This command will create a new subshell.

$ echo $$

1678

This is the process ID of the newly created subshell.

$ echo $name

Nothing will be displayed, as the local variables from the parent shell are not inherited in the newly created child shell

116

or subshell:

$ exit

We will exit the subshell and return to the original shell terminal.

$ echo $$

1234

This is the process ID of the current shell or parent shell.

$ echo $name
Rob Jonson

This is displaying the variable's presence in the original shell.

Variables created in the current shell will not be available in a subshell or child shell. If we need to use a variable in a child shell, then we need to export them using the export command.

- **Exporting variables**

Using the export command will help us to make variables available in the child process or subshell. But if we declare new variables in the child process and export it in the child process, the variable will not be available in the parent process. The parent process can export variables to a child, but the child process cannot export variables to the parent process.

. Whenever we create a Shell script and execute it, a new shell process is created and the Shell script runs in that process. Any exported variable values are available to the new shell or to any sub-process.

We can export any variable as follows:

$ export NAME

Or:

$ declare -x NAME

Let's understand the concept of exporting the variable by the following example:

$ PERSON=" Rob Jonson "
$ export PERSON
$ echo $PERSON
Rob Jonson
$ echo $$

515

The process ID of the current shell or parent shell is 515. **$ bash** This will start a subshell. **$ echo $$**

555

This is the process ID of new or subshell.

$ echo $PERSON
Rob Jonson

119

$ PERSON="Author"
$ echo $PERSON
Author
$ exit

This will terminate the subshell and will be placed in the parent shell.

$ echo $$

515

This is the process ID of the parent shell.

$ echo $PERSON
Author

- **Working with read-only variables**

During Shell scripting, we may need a few variables, which cannot be modified. This may be needed for security reasons. We can declare variables as read-only using following command read-only:

The usage is as follows:

$ readonly currency=Dollars
Let's try to remove the variable:

$ unset currency
bash: unset: currency: cannot unset: readonly variable
If we try to change or remove the ready-only variable in the script, it will give the following error:

```
#!/bin/bash
AUTHOR="Rob Jonson"
readonly AUTHOR
AUTHOR="Rob"
```
This would produce the following result:

/bin/sh: AUTHOR: This variable is read only.
Another technique:

```
Declare -r variable=1
echo "variable=$variable"
(( var1++ ))
```
Output after execution of the script:

line 4: variable: readonly variable

- **Working with command line arguments (special variables, set and shift, getopt)**

Command line arguments are required for the following reasons:

-They inform the utility or command as to which file or group of files to process (reading/writing of files)

-Command line arguments tell the command/utility which option to use.

Check the following command line:

- **student@ubuntu:~$ my_program arg1 arg2 arg3**

If my_command is a bash Shell script, then we can access every command line positional parameters inside the script as follows:

- $0 would contain "my_program" # Command
- $1 would contain "arg1"
- $2 would contain "arg2"

122

- $3 would contain "arg3"
- # First parameter
- # Second parameter
- # Third parameter

The following is the summary of positional parameters:

0	Shell script name or command
1 – $ 9	Positional parameters 1–9

{
1
0
}
	Positional parameter 10

#	Total number of parameters

*	Evaluates to all the positional parameters	
@	Same as $*, except when double quoted	
$ * "	Displays all parameters as "$1 $2 $3", and so on	
$ @ "	Displays all parameters as "$1" "$2" "$3", and so on	

Let's create a script param.sh as follows:

```
#!/bin/bash
echo "Total number of parameters are = $#"
echo "Script name = $0"
echo "First Parameter is $1"
echo "Second Parameter is $2"
echo "Third Parameter is $3"
```

echo "Fourth Parameter is $4"
echo "Fifth Parameter is $5"
echo "All parameters are = $*"

Then as usual, give execute permission to script and then execute it:

./parameter.sh London Washington Delhi Dhaka Paris

Output:

Total number of parameters are = 5
Command is = ./parameter.sh
First Parameter is London

Second Parameter is Washington
Third Parameter is Delhi
Fourth Parameter is Dhaka
Fifth Parameter is Paris
All parameters are = London Washington Delhi Dhaka Paris

Understanding set

Many times we may not pass arguments on the command line, but we may need to set parameters internally inside the script.

We can declare parameters by the set command as follows:

$ set USA Canada UK France
$ echo $1
USA
$ echo $2
Canada
$ echo $3
UK
$ echo $4
France

We can use this inside the set_01.sh script as follows:

```
#!/bin/bash
set USA Canada UK France
echo $1
echo $2
echo $3
```

echo $4

Run the script as:

$ ./set.sh

Output:

USA
Canada
UK
France

Table declare Options	
Option	**Meaning**
−a	An array will be created
−f	Displays function names and definitions
−F	Displays only the function names
−	Makes variables integer

i	types
r ⁻	Makes variables read-only
x ⁻	Exports variables

We give commands as follows:

set One Two Three Four Five
echo \$0
echo \$1
echo \$2
echo \$*
echo \$#
echo \${10} \${11}   # Use this syntax
for parameters for 10th and
          # 11th parameters
Let us write script set_02.sh as follows:

```
#!/bin/bash
echo The date is $(date)
set $(date)
echo The month is $2
exit 0
```

Output:

```
student@ubuntu:~/Desktop/work$ bash set_02.sh
The date is Thu Apr 23 00:36:53 IST 2015
The month is Apr
student@ubuntu:~/Desktop/work$ 
```

Resetting positional parameters

In certain situations, we may need to reset original positional parameters. Let's try the following: **set Rob Jonson** This will reset the positional parameters.

Now $1 is Alan, $2 is John, and $3 is Dennis. Inside the scripts, we can save positional parameters in a variable as follows: **oldargs=$***

Then, we can set new positional parameters. Later on, we can bring back our original positional parameters as follows:

set $oldargs

- **Creating an array and initializing it**

129

You will learn about creating an array in the Bash shell. If the array name is FRUIT, then we can create an array as follows: **FRUIT[index]=value**

– Index is the integer value. It should be 0 or any positive integer value. We can also   create an array as follows:

- **$ declare -a array_name**
- **$ declare -a arrayname=(value1 value2 value3)**
    - **$ declare -a fruit=('Mango' 'Banana' 'Apple' 'Orange' 'Papaya')**
    - **$ declare -a array_name=(word1 word2 word3 ...)**
    - **$ declare -a fruit=(Pears Apple Mango Banana Papaya)**
    - **$ echo ${fruit[0]}**
    - **Pears**
    - **$ echo ${fruit[1]}**
    - **Apple**
    - **$ echo "All the fruits are ${fruit[*]}"**
    All the fruits are Pears Apple Mango Banana Papaya

- **$ echo "The number of elements in the array are ${#fruit[*]}"**
- **The number of elements in the array are 3**
- **$ unset fruit or unset ${fruit[*]}**

Chapter 6 : Tips and Tricks with with shell scripting

In the last chapter, we talked about shell and environment variables. You also learned about how to export environment variables, read-only variables, command-line arguments.

In this chapter, we will cover following topics:

- Interactive Shell scripts and reading from the keyboard.

- Using the here operator (<<) and here string (<<<)

131

- File handling.

- Enabling debugging.

- Syntax checking.

  - **Interactive Shell scripts – reading user input**

    The read command is a shell built-in command for reading data from a file or keyboard. The read command receives the input from the keyboard or a le until it receives a newline character. Then, it converts the newline character into a null character:

    1. Read a value and store it in the variable, shown as follows:

    read variable
    echo $variable

    This will receive a text from the keyboard. The received text will be stored in the variable.

2. Command read with prompt. Whenever we need to display the prompt with certain text, we use the –p option. The option -p displays the text that is placed after –p on the screen:

```
#!/bin/bash
```

following line will print "Enter value: " and then read data.

The received text will be stored in variable value.

```
read -p "Enter value :  " value
```

Output:
Enter value : abcd

3. If the variable name is not supplied next to the read command, then the received data or text will be stored in a special built-in variable called REPLY. Let's write a simple script read_01.sh, shown as follows:

```bash
#!/bin/bash
echo "Where do you stay ?"
read      # we have not supplied
any option or variable
echo "You stay in $REPLY"
```

Save the file, give the permission to execute, and run the script as follows:

$ chmod u+x read_01.sh
$ ./read_01.sh

Output:

"Where do you stay?"
Las Vegas
"You stay at Las Vegas"

4. We will write the script read_02.sh. This script prompts the user to enter their rst and last name to greet the user with their full name:

```bash
#!/bin/bash
echo "Enter first Name"
read FIRSTNAME
```

```
echo "Enter Last Name"
read LASTNAME
NAME="$FIRSTNAME
$LASTNAME"
echo "Name is $NAME"
```

5. For reading text and storing in multiple variables, the syntax is as follows:

$ read value1 value2 value3

Let's write Shell script read_03.sh, shown as follows:

```
#!/bin/bash
echo "What is your name?"
read fname mname lname
echo "Your first name is : $fname"
echo "Your middle name is : $mname"
echo "Your last name is : $lname"
```

Save the file, give the permission to execute, and run the script as follows:

```
What is your name?
Rob Richard Jonson
```

"Your first name is : Rob"
"Your middle name is : Richard"
"Your last name is : Jonson"

6. Let's learn about reading a list of words and storing them in an array:
   ```
   #!/bin/bash
   echo -n "Name few cities? "
   read -a cities
   echo "Name    of    city    is $cities[2]."
   ```

Save the file, give the permission to execute, and run the script as follows:
       Name few cities? Delhi London Washington Tokyo
       Name of city is Washington.

In this case, the list of cities is stored in the array of cities. The elements in the array are here:
   cities[0] = Delhi
   cities[1] = London
   cities[2] = Washington
   cities[3] = Tokyo

The index of the array starts with 0, and in this case, it ends at 3. In this case, four elements are added in the cities[] array.

8. If we want the user to press the Enter key, then we can use the read command along with one unused variable, shown as follows:

Echo "Please press enter to proceed further "

read temp
echo "Now backup operation will be started! "

- **The here document and the << operator**

It is a special type of block of text or code. It is also a special form of I/O redirection. It can be used to feed the command list to an interactive program.

137

The syntax of the usage of the here document or the << operator is as follows:

command << HERE
text1 .....
text 2....

HERE

This tells the shell that the command should receive the data from a current source, such as the here document until the pattern is received. In this case, the pattern is the word "HERE". We have used the delimiter as HERE. We can use any other word as the delimiter, such as quite or nish. All the text reads up to a pattern; or the HERE text is used as an input for a command. The text or file received by the command is known as the HERE document:

$ cat << QUIT
> first input line
> ...
> last input line
> QUIT

The block of text inserted after and before QUIT will be treated as a file. This content will be given as input to the command cat. We will also see more examples of various other commands, such as sort, wc, and similar.

Let's write the script here_01.sh:

```
#!/bin/bash
cat << quit
  Command is $0
  First Argument is $1
  Second Argument is $2

Quit
```

Save the file, give execute permission and run the script as follows:
$ chmod here_01.sh
$./here_01.sh Monday Tuesday
Output:

Command is here_01.sh
First Argument is Monday
Second Argument is Tuesday

The text block created in the preceding

139

script between the quit words is known as the here document. We can treat this here document as a separate document. It can also be treated as multiple line input redirected to a Shell script.

The here operator with the wc command

Let's write a script for using the wc command along with the here document:

1. Create Shell script here_03.sh:

```
#!/bin/bash

wc -w << EOF

There was major earthquake

On May 13, 2017

in India.

There was a huge loss of human life in this tragic event in India.

EOF
```

2. Save the le, give the permission to execute, and run the script as follows:

$ chmod u+x here_03.sh

$ ./here_03.sh

3. The output is here:

21

In this script, we have used the here document as an input for the wc command to calculate the number of words:

Tape backup using << here operator

Let's write a script for taking the tape backup by using the tar command and the here document:

Let's write the script here_04.sh:

#!/bin/bash

We have used tar utility for archiving home folder on tape

```
          tar -cvf /dev/st0 /home/student
2>/dev/null
          # store status of tar operation
in variable status
          [  $?  -eq  0  ]  &&
status="Success" || status="Failed"
          # Send email to administrator
          mail  -s  'Backup  status'
ganesh@levanatech.com                 <<
End_Of_Message
          The backup job finished.
          End date: $(date)
          Status : $status
          End_Of_Message
```

Save the le, give the permission to execute, and run the script as follows:

$ chmod u+x here_04.sh

$ ./here_04.sh

This script uses the tar command to archive the home folder in the tape device, and then it sends mail to an administrator using the command mail. We have used the here document to feed data into the command mail.

The utility ed and here operator

The ed is a basic type of editor. We can edit text les using this editor:

1. Write the script here_05.sh:

```
#!/bin/bash
# flowers.txt contains the name of flowers
cat flowers.txt
ed flowers.txt << quit
,s/Rose/Lily/g
w
q
quit
cat flowers.txt
```

Save the le, give the permission to execute, and run the script as follows:

$ chmod u+x here_05.sh

$ ./here_05.sh

The output is here:

Aster, Daffodil, Daisy, Jasmin, Lavender, Rose, Sunflower

59
59

Aster, Daffodil, Daisy, Jasmin, Lavender, Lily, Sunflower

In this script, we have used passed the here document to the utility for editing the le flowers.txt. We replaced the Rose word with Lily.

The here string and the <<< operator

The here string is used for input redirection from text or a variable. Input is

144

mentioned on the same line within single quotes (").

The syntax is as follows:

$ command <<< 'string'

Let's see the following example hereString_01.sh:

#!/bin/bash

wc –w <<< 'Good Morning and have a nice day !'

Save the le, give the permission, and run the script as follows:

$ chmod u+x hereString_01.sh

$ ./hereString_01.sh

Here is the output:

8

In this example, the string Good Morning and have a nice day! Is called as the here string.

Using exec to assign le descriptor (fd) to le

In the Bash shell environment, every process has three les opened by default. These are standard input, display, and error. The le descriptors associated with them are 0, 1, and 2 respectively. In the Bash shell, we can assign the le descriptor to any input or output le. These are called le descriptors.

The syntax for declaring output.txt as output is as follows:

exec fd > output.txt

This command will declare the number fd as an output le descriptor. The syntax for closing the le is as follows:

exec fd<&-

To close fd, which is 5, enter the following:

exec 5<&-

We will try to understand these concepts by writing scripts.

Understanding reading from a file

Let's write a script to read from a le: Write the script file_02.sh, shown as follows:

```
#!/bin/bash
# We will open file sample_input.txt
for reading purpose.
# We are assigning descriptor 3 to the
file.
exec 3< sample_input.txt
cat <&3
# Closing file
exec 3<&-
```

Save the le, give the permission to execute, and run the script as follows:

$ chmod u+x file_02.sh

147

We will create the sample_input.txt le as follows: **$ echo "Hello to All" > sample_input.txt** Run the script and check the result: **$ ./file_02.sh**

Output:

Hello to All

Understanding reading and writing to a file

In the earlier examples, we opened the le either for reading or writing. Now, we will see how to open the le for reading and writing purposes:

exec fd<> fileName

If the le descriptor number is not specified, then 0 will be used in its place. The le will be created if it does not exist.

This procedure is useful to update les.

Let's understand following script. Write the Shell script file_03.sh as follows:

```
#!/bin/bash
file_name="sample_out.txt"
# We are assing fd number 3 to file.
# We will be doing read and write
operations on file
exec 3<> $file_name
# Writing to file
echo """

Do not dwell in the past,
do not dream of the future,
concentrate the mind on the present
moment. - Buddha
""" >&3
# closing file with fd number 3
exec 3>&-
```

Using command read on file descriptor (fd)

We can use command read to get data from a le to store it in variables. The procedure for using the read command to get a text from a le is as follows:

read -u fd variable1 variable2 ... variableN

- ## File handling – reading line by line

You will learn how to use the while loop and the read command to read a le line by line. You will learn more about the while loop in the upcoming chapters.

Let's write the script file_07.sh, shown as follows:

```
#!/bin/bash
echo "Enter the name of file for reading"
read file_name
exec<$file_name
while read var_line
do
  echo $var_line
done
```

For executing the preceding script, we will need to create a le with some text in it. Then, we will pass this le name for reading purposes.

- **Debugging**

In the very old days of computer technology, the initial problems with computers were due to real insects. Due to this, fault nding was later called as nding a bug. Therefore, the process of nding and xing the problem in computers was called debugging.

The process of debugging involves the following:

-Finding out what has gone wrong

-Fixing the problem   In the actual

debugging process, you will need to do the following:

- Understand the error message and find out what is the problem with the script.

- Find the error location in the script.

- Locate the line number from the error message. The following are a few error messages: ° debug_sp: line 11: [7: command not found] ° file: line 6: unexpected EOF while looking for matching `"' These messages inform the user about the line numbers of the script which contain errors.

- Correct the issue or problematic part of the code. We may have to read the line as well as look backward from this line number for any possible reason for the error.

Debugging mode – disabling the shell (option -n)

In the Bash shell, the -n option is a shortcut for **noexec** (as in no execution). This option tells the shell to not run the commands. Instead, the shell just checks for syntax errors. We can test the script as follows:

$ bash –n hello.sh

The –n option will tell the Bash shell to check the syntax in the Shell script; but not to execute the Shell script. Another way to do this is as follows:

#!/bin/bash -n

We have modified shebang line.

In this case, we can test the Shell script as follows:

$ chmod u+x hello.sh
$ ./hello.sh

This option is safe, since the shell commands are not executed. We can catch incomplete if, for, while, case, and similar programming constructs as well as much more syntactical errors.

Let's write debug_01.sh: #!/bin/bash

echo -n "Commands in bin directory are : $var"
for var in $(ls)
do
        echo -n -e "$var   "
do
no error if "done" is typed instead of "do"

Save the le, give the permission to execute, and run the script as follows:

$ chmod u+x debug_01.sh
$ ./debug_01.sh
Output:

Commands in bin directory are :
./hello.sh: line 7: syntax error near
    unexpected token `do'
    ./hello.sh: line 7: `do'

$ bash –n debug_01.sh
Output:

**hello.sh: line 7: syntax error near
unexpected token `do'
hello.sh: line 7: `do'**

Debugging mode – the tracing execution (option -x)

The -x option, short for **xtrace** or execution trace, tells the shell to echo each command after performing the substitution steps. Thus, we will see the value of variables and commands.

We can trace the execution of the Shell script as follows:

$ bash –x hello.sh

Instead of the previous way, we can modify the shebang line as follows:

#!/bin/bash -x Let's test the earlier script debug_01.sh as follows: **$ bash –x hello.sh** Output:

$ bash –x debug_02.sh
+ echo Hello student
Hello student
+ date
+ echo The date is Fri May 1 00:18:52 IST 2015
The date is Fri May 1 00:18:52 IST 2015
+ echo Your home shell is /bin/bash
Your home shell is /bin/bash
+ echo Good-bye student
Good-bye student

Summarizing the debugging options for the Bash shell

The following is a summary of various debugging options used for debugging, such as -x, -v, and -n with their details:

**$ bash −n script_name //
interpretation without execution**

**$ bash −v script_name // Display
commands in script**

**$ bash −x script_name // Trace the
execution of script**

**$ bash −xv script_name // Enable
options x and v for debugging**

**$ bash +xv script_name //Disable
options x and v for debugging**

Using the set command

Most of the time, we invoke the
debugging mode from the rst line of the
script. This debugging mode will remain
active until the last line of code. But many
times, we may need to enable debugging
for a particular section of the script. By
using the set command, we can enable and
disable debugging at any point in our
Shell script:

set -x
section of script
set +x
Consider the following script:
#!/bin/bash

```
str1="USA"
str2="Canada";
[ $str1 = $str2 ]
echo $?
Set –x
[ $str1 != $str2 ]
echo $?
[ -z $str1 ]
echo $?
```